Simón Bolívar

The Liberator

Frank de Varona

SCHOLASTIC INC.

New York   Toronto   London   Auckland   Sydney
Mexico City   New Delhi   Hong Kong   Buenos Aires

Illustrations
Greg Copeland

Developed by ONO Books in cooperation with Scholastic Inc.

ISBN 0-439-59787-0

2 3 4 5 6 7 8 9 10   23   12 11 10 09 08 07 06 05 04

Contents

Welcome to This Book

If you had a dream, would you fight for it? Would you give up your friends? Would you give up your money? Would you risk your life?

Simón Bolívar had a dream. He believed in freedom for the people of South America. He wanted South America to be free from Spanish rule. He fought more than 200 battles for this belief. He lost his home, his money, and his friends.

But was it worth the fight? Was he able to make his dream come true?

Target Words

These words will help you understand what Bolívar was fighting for.

- **ideal:** a dream of something that is perfect

  Freedom was Simón's ideal.

- **liberate:** to set free

  Simón hoped to liberate South America from Spanish rule.

- **revolution:** an uprising by the people of a country to change their government

  Simón fought a long revolution to get the Spanish out of South America.

Reader Tips

Here's how to get the most out of this book.

- **Maps** Maps can help you locate the places you read about in the story of Simón's life. As you read, check out the map on page 11 to find the places Simón helped to gain their freedom.

- **Sequence of Events** As you read, look for signal words such as *before, next, finally,* and *last.* These words will help you keep track of what happens in Simón's life. As you read, look for signal words and important dates to understand when events in Simón's life took place.

Wild Child

Simón Bolívar's family had money, but not power.

In 1783, Venezuela was not a country yet. It was a **colony** in South America. It was one of the colonies ruled by Spain. The other colonies were ruled by Portugal.

Most of the people who lived in Venezuela were **Creoles.** A Creole is a person who was born in South America but whose **ancestors** were born in Spain. That difference may seem small. But it wasn't to the Spaniards. They thought that people born in Spain were better than Creoles.

So the Spaniards made a lot of rules. Only the Spanish were allowed to have important jobs in the government. Only the Spanish were allowed to have top jobs in the army. The Creoles were not allowed to have power of any kind.

The Creoles were treated unfairly. But the Native South Americans were treated worse. Many of them were slaves. They had to work on **plantations** for no money. And they couldn't go to school or live where they wanted.

Over the years, there were many Creoles and Native Venezuelans who spoke out. They said that Venezuela should be free from Spanish rule. Some even tried to fight for their freedom. But each time, the Spanish won and the freedom fighters were hung. So most just gave up.

On July 24, 1783, a Creole boy was born in Venezuela. He would become a great leader. He would free the Spanish colonies of South America. His name was Simón Bolívar.

The Boy Who Had Everything

Simón Bolívar's family was rich. They had a mansion in the city. They had a country house, too. It was only a few miles away. There, they had a river filled with fish and miles of beautiful gardens. Wild horses ran free on their land.

The Bolívars were so rich that they didn't even know exactly how much land they owned.

Simón rode wild horses at his family's country house.

The Bolívars were treated better than most Creoles because they had so much money. So Simón never had any idea that he was being treated unfairly.

Simón spent **carefree** days chasing the wild horses he loved so much. But by the time Simón turned nine, both of his parents were dead. He went to live in the city with his Uncle Palacios. Life was very different there.

Simón's uncle hired religious teachers for the boy. They were very strict. Simón spent long hours studying. He was allowed to read only certain books. Simón was very unhappy. Then one day, for a reason that no one knows, Simón's uncle fired these teachers.

The next day, a new teacher appeared. His name was Simón Rodríguez. He was twenty-three years old. This new teacher would change Simón Bolívar's life again....

Heads Up!

Describe Simón in your own words. What do you think he was like when he got older?

Who Rules?

Before the 1500s, Native South Americans ruled their own land. Then during the 1500s, European explorers sailed across the Atlantic Ocean. They discovered North and South America. They called it the New World.

The Europeans decided that they wanted this land. They fought and killed many native people. Many more native people died from the diseases the Europeans brought with them.

By the 1700s, England and Spain held most of North America. Spain and Portugal ruled most of South America. See the map at right. That's how South America was divided up.

By this time, many **generations** of Europeans had been born in the New World. But they didn't think of themselves as Europeans anymore. And so they didn't want to take orders from Europe.

In 1776, the American colonies had a **revolution.** They kicked the British out and formed the United States. Bolívar wanted to do the same. He wanted to kick the Spanish out of South America and form a free country.

This is what South America looked like in the 1700s.

Life Lessons

Simón changed from a spoiled brat into a serious student.

Simón's new teacher was full of **passion** and fire. Rodríguez was the most passionate about freedom. He didn't think Spain should rule the colony of Venezuela. He thought the Creoles should make their own laws. He also thought it was wrong to make the Native Venezuelans slaves. He had ideas about everything. And he wanted to share them with Simón.

But Rodríguez soon realized that his student was a spoiled rich kid. He needed to grow up a little before he could understand these ideas.

So Rodríguez took Bolívar to the countryside. They lived simply without fancy clothes or manners. They hiked mountains. They swam in rivers. They chased wild horses.

For Simón, it was a dream come true. It reminded him of happy times he spent in the country before his parents died.

Then, Rodríguez began to talk to Bolívar about freedom. He taught the young boy history. He explained how the Spanish took over the Americas and made slaves of the native people. Simón learned all about governments and **democracy**. Rodríguez told him that people should be able to choose their own leaders and make their own laws. And they should be willing to fight for their rights.

A Warning

Rodríguez took a big risk talking that way. Anyone who spoke out against the Spaniards got in trouble.

At that time, Venezuelan **rebels** were fighting the Spaniards. But they were losing. When the Spanish caught the rebels, they killed them—

---**Heads Up!**---

How did having Rodríguez as a tutor change Bolívar?

or worse. Sometimes, they chopped off the heads, arms, and legs of the rebels. Sometimes, the Spaniards left the bodies of the rebels in iron cages in town squares. In that way, the Spanish army could send a message to others. "If you rise up against us this will happen to you, too."

One day, a Spanish officer heard Rodríguez say he wanted to throw the Spanish out of Venezuela. He said Rodríguez was **disloyal.** He called Rodríguez a rebel.

Simón heard what had happened. "Is this true, Rodríguez?" he asked.

Rodríguez set his jaw. "All people deserve to be free," he said.

"Are you willing to risk your life to help others be free?" Simón asked.

Rodríguez looked at his student. "What kind of a man would I be if I wasn't?" Then he answered his own question. "No man at all."

But Rodríguez knew he would be hanged if he stayed. The next day, Rodríguez left Venezuela.

Simón **admired** what Rodríguez was doing. He knew his teacher would keep up the fight wherever he went. Still, Bolívar was very sad. He was losing both a teacher and a good friend.

Seeds of Revolt

Bolívar stood up for Venezuela.

Simón's uncle got him another tutor. But no one could replace Rodríguez. Simón lost interest in his studies. So at the age of 16, Simón's uncle sent him to Spain with another uncle, Mallo.

Uncle Mallo was very rich. He loved parties and was a close friend of the Queen of Spain. Simón played tennis with the Prince of Spain. He read great books. And he married. Her name was Maria. And she and Simón were very much in love.

When Simón was nineteen, he and Maria returned to Venezuela to live in Simón's childhood home. They were very happy. But six months later, Maria died of yellow fever. Simón did not think he would ever recover from Maria's death. He said he would never marry again. He kept his word.

Simón went back to Europe to forget his pain. He went to parties. He traveled. He met kings and princes. He also met other people who believed in democracy.

Simón watched the rulers of Europe. He saw how they kept all the power for themselves. Simón thought this was unfair. He wanted a better life for the people of South America.

In the summer of 1805, Simón heard that Rodríguez was in Europe, too. He made plans to meet up with his old friend.

They hiked through Italy together. As they walked, they talked about current events. France had just **invaded** Spain. The French had put one of their own men on the Spanish throne. Spain was weak now. Maybe the time was right to force Spain out of South America. Simón thought it was. And he wanted to lead the way.

One night in August, Simón and Rodríguez climbed a hill outside Rome, Italy. Simón looked out on the lights of the city.

"I **swear** before the God of my fathers," he said. "My arm shall not rest until I have broken the chains that **bind** us!"

Simón promised to free the part of South America that was controlled by Spain.

Visiting the United States

Two years later, Simón left Europe. On his way home, he visited the United States. There, he saw a young democracy in action. People had fought for their freedom. They could vote and make decisions about their country. Simón wanted the same for South America.

When he returned home, Simón began talking to friends about revolution. He told them that freeing Venezuela would be the first step in **liberating** all of South America. Simón was determined to make his dream come true.

One night, Simón went to a party at the home of a Spanish **governor.** The guests were toasting the king of Spain. Then it was Simón's turn. He raised his glass high.

"I lift my glass for the happiness of the king," he said. "However, I raise it even higher for the freedom of Venezuela!"

The Spanish governor was angry. From that day on, he had Simón watched. And for good reason. Simón had formed a secret group of rebels called the Patriot Society. He also helped rebel fighters form an army. Simón was their general.

In 1810, Simón and an army general named Francisco de Miranda went to war. They attacked the Spanish in Caracas, Venezuela—and won!

Simón and Miranda gathered the rebels together. They spoke about their **ideals.**

"Let us lay the cornerstone of American freedom without fear."

They signed a paper. In it, they said that Venezuela would now be free from Spain. This paper was like the United States Declaration of Independence.

But the Spanish did not want Venezuela to have independence. They attacked the small rebel army and took back control of Venezuela.

The Spanish soldiers caught Miranda and sent him to prison in Spain. Simón escaped. He went into **exile.** He fled to New Granada (now called Colombia).

Many thought that Simón's days as a revolutionary were over. They were wrong.

—Heads Up!—
What happened to turn Bolívar into a revolutionary?

Death March

Would they survive long enough to fight?

The years went by. Simón's dream of a united South America was stronger then ever. He became the leader of a small patriot army in New Granada. Over the years, that small army grew.

In 1813, Simón and his army attacked Caracas, Venezuela, again. And again, the rebels won control of the city. But by the next year, the Spanish had taken it right back again.

The rebels weren't getting anywhere. They needed help.

Then, in 1815, Simón went to Haiti. The small country had recently freed itself from France's rule. The president of Haiti agreed to give Simón money to help him fight the Spanish.

Simón called for a "War to the Death." South America would be free from the Spanish at last.

Simón led his army up a cold mountain.

But even with help from Haiti, the battle for freedom did not go well. Simón and his men were outnumbered by the Spanish. There seemed no way for them to take control of Venezuela.

Simón needed a new plan. He decided to go to New Granada. The rebel army would **launch** a surprise attack over the Andes Mountains. No one would expect it because it couldn't be done!

Rough Mud and Ice

In May 1819, Simón and about 2,500 fighters left Venezuela. It was the rainy season. For seven days, they marched in water up to their waists. They held their guns high to keep them dry.

In June, Simón and his men reached the Andes. Icy mountains rose two miles high in front of them. On the other side lay New Granada. If they turned back now, Simón would have to give up his dream.

For four days Simón and his men climbed higher and higher on the icy paths. Their clothes were not warm enough. They ran out of food. One by one their horses froze to death. Would they be next?

Facing the Spanish

Could a small, weak group of rebels beat the Spanish army?

At last, Simón's army came down the other side of the mountains. They had reached New Granada. But they were cold and hungry and tired. More than 1,000 men had died. Even worse, they had very few rifles left. They would have to fight with **lances** and knives.

The Spanish army was camped outside Bogotá, the capital city of New Grenada. They were guarding an important bridge. On the night of August 5, the rebel fighters surprised the Spanish troops.

The two armies fought hard. Then a storm struck. The Spaniards took cover in their forts. But the rebel army was caught in the driving rain. They were forced to leave.

"It's not over yet," Simón said. "We've made a good start. Tomorrow we will finish the job."

The next day, Simón and his men returned. They attacked the Spanish army at the bridge. The rebels were outnumbered but they fought bravely. They forced the Spanish to give up. This battle was an important victory.

The next day, Simón led his troops into Bogotá. He and his men took the city from the Spaniards. New Granada was free.

Simón's dream was to create a new country in South America. It would be a free, united country won from the Spanish. He would call this country the Republic of Colombia, or Gran Colombia. It would include New Granada, Venezuela, and Quito (now called Equador).

Now, all Simón had to do was liberate Venezuela and Quito.

Heads Up!

Why do you think Bolívar's men fought so hard at the bridge? Think about what they had already been through and why.

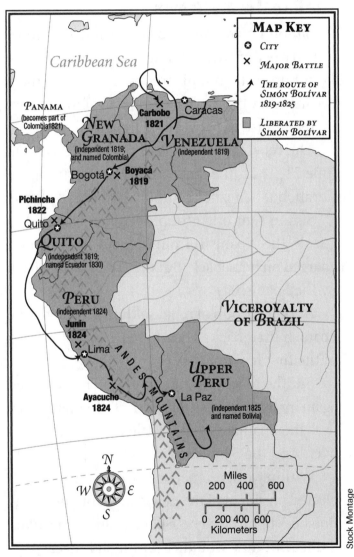

MAP KEY

⊗ CITY

✕ MAJOR BATTLE

↱ THE ROUTE OF
SIMÓN BOLÍVAR
1819–1825

▨ LIBERATED BY
SIMÓN BOLÍVAR

Caribbean Sea

PANAMA
(becomes part of
Colombia1821)

NEW
GRANADA
(independent 1819;
and named Colombia)

VENEZUELA
(independent 1819)

Carbobo
1821

Caracas

Bogotá ⊗ ✕ Boyacá
1819

Pichincha
1822

Quito ✕⊗

QUITO
(independent 1819;
named Ecuador 1830)

PERU
(independent 1824)

Junín
1824

✕⊗ Lima

A N D E S   M O U N T A I N S

Ayacucho
1824

VICEROYALTY
OF BRAZIL

UPPER
PERU

⊗ La Paz
(independent 1825
and named Bolivia)

N
W ✦ E
S

Miles
0   200   400   600

0   200 400 600
Kilometers

Stock Montage

**Use this map to follow along as Simón helps to free
South America.**

The Rebel Army Grows

Simón Bolívar went to war again. This time, he had a real army. More than 4,000 soldiers came from Europe to join his troops. Some were there because they believed in democracy. Others were there because they hated the Spanish.

The rebel army now had 6,500 soldiers. On June 21, 1821, they met 5,000 Spanish troops in Carabobo, Venezuela. But it was a bloody fight.

Simón sent one group of soldiers around to attack the Spanish from behind. The rebels charged on horseback. But they were beaten back by the Spanish.

Another group of rebel soldiers attacked. The Spanish fired back. They killed 17 rebel officers in the first few minutes.

But the rebels did not give up. They charged again on horseback with lances. Then finally, they beat the Spaniards. The Battle of Carabobo was over. And the Spanish army was on the run.

Within weeks, Venezuela was free. Simón was elected president of the new nation. But he wasn't finished fighting. The Spanish still controlled Quito. But they wouldn't for much longer.

Spaniards, Go Home!

Simón was worn out. But the patriots still needed him. Could he say no?

Simón and his troops marched hundreds of miles through Quito. They fought as they marched. They freed city after city.

South Americans called Bolívar El Liberator (The Liberator). They cheered loudly whenever they saw him.

In one town, the people had planned a special way to honor Simón. A ten-year-old girl stood in the town square to give a speech. But when she opened her mouth, no words would come. Her knees shook and her mind went blank.

Simón smiled and put his hand on the girl's shoulder. "Don't worry," he told her. "Sometimes I lose my courage, too. But then I remember what I'm fighting for. And my courage comes back!"

The people cheered and clapped. But Simón and his men were soon on their way.

Simón and his soldiers freed Quito from Spanish rule. The people threw roses in the streets. They praised Simón as a hero.

One More Battle

"Now, I'm ready to go home," Simón said. "I want to enjoy the freedom I have fought for."

But the patriots begged Simón to keep fighting. If the Spanish stayed in power in Peru, they would always be a threat. They might try to regain control of the countries that were free. And the patriots knew that without Simón's help, the Spanish would never leave Peru.

Simón couldn't ignore the patriots of Peru. He sent some of his troops to help them fight. But Simón's troops came right back. The army in Peru said they didn't want Simón's help. They wanted to win their war on their own.

But the Peruvians lost two important battles to the Spaniards. Many soldiers were killed. The army realized that they did need Simón. And once more Simón came to help.

Once more Simón went into battle.

In August 1824, Simón's troops met the Spanish at Junin, Peru. The rebels won the battle in less than an hour.

Four months later, Peru was free. Patriots in Upper Peru wanted to form their own country. And they wanted to honor the man who had helped them. They split from Peru and gave their country a new name. They called it Bolivia after Simón Bolívar.

Heads Up!

Bolívar helped to free four countries. Name them in the order they were freed.

End of a Dream

Had it all been for nothing?

Simón returned to the country now called Colombia. Everyone said he was a hero. For a time, Simón enjoyed the life he had fought for.

But Simón wasn't satisfied. His dream was to bring all the free South American countries together. He wanted one nation—much like the United States. But that turned out to be even harder to do than fighting the Spanish.

The patriots fought bitterly among themselves. They couldn't agree on who their leaders should be. When one group came to power, it would kill all the **rival** groups.

Simón watched his dream fade. He gave up on democracy. He led his troops against the countries he helped create. He said that he would be leader of them all.

The people began to call him a **dictator**. They thought he might be as bad as the Spanish.

The Hunt for Bolívar

One morning, Simón woke up to the sound of shouts and gunfire. The noise was coming from outside his window. There was a mob of people. "Death to Bolívar!" they shouted.

"Quick!" said Manuela, Simón's girlfriend. "Climb out the window. Go!"

"But why?" Simón said. "I don't understand. I helped these people. I gave them freedom. Why have they turned against me?"

"Go!" Manuela said again. "They're breaking down the door!"

Simón did what she said. Then Manuela grabbed Simón's sword and opened the front door.

"What are you doing?" she cried. "Why do you wake up a tired woman?"

Heads Up!

Look up the word dictator *in the glossary. Was Simón a dictator? Do you think that he was as bad as the Spanish? Explain.*

Manuela helped Simón escape.

"We want Simón Bolívar," a man from the crowd screamed. "Where is he?"

"He's not here," Manuela said.

Another man looked into the back room. "Then why is the window open?"

"I heard noises in the street," Manuela said. "I looked outside to see what it was. You fools woke me up. I should be sleeping!"

The mob got mad. They pushed into the house. They ripped Manuela's sword away from her. They beat her up.

But Manuela's plan had worked. It gave Simón time to escape. Simón remained in hiding for six hours. Then he found a group of loyal men. They attacked the mob that had come after him.

Simón was upset and confused by what had happened. He'd beaten the Spanish. And were the people happy? No. Were they peaceful? No. They were even turning against him. This was not what he had fought for.

Soon after, there was more bad news. Simón learned that a top rebel general had been killed. It was a terrible shock. The general was a close friend of Simón's. He had shown great courage throughout the revolution.

Simón was having trouble sleeping. He was worn out. Then he got sick. He caught a fever that wouldn't go away. He left the city to get some rest. But his sickness grew worse. Some days, he could hardly breathe.

Simón Bolívar died on December 17, 1830. His dream of turning South America into one nation never came true.

Today, Bolívar is viewed as a hero in South America. His picture is on money and stamps. Statues of him can be found in many town squares. And his birthday is a national holiday in Venezuela and Bolivia.

Heads Up!

In 1824, Bolívar had freed half of South America. In 1830, he died broken and unhappy. What happened in those six years to make him miserable?

Love of His Life

Simón was in love with freedom. But he had another love, as well. Her name was Manuela Sáenz. She was as fearless as he was. She fought as a **colonel** in the rebel army. She talked politics. She wasn't afraid to tell Bolívar what to do. And he was madly in love with her.

When Simón died, many people hated him. People thought he had been disloyal to the revolution. And they hated Manuela, too.

After Simón's death, Manuela was kicked out of Colombia. She died in Peru 25 years later. She was very poor. Her love letters from Simón were burned. Not long after Bolívar's death, people started to say he was a hero again. Today, people finally see Manuela as a hero, too.

Glossary

admire *(verb)* to think highly of someone or something (p. 14)

ancestor *(noun)* a member of your family who lived a long time ago (p. 6)

bind *(verb)* to tie up, restrict (p. 16)

carefree *(adjective)* having no worries (p. 9)

colonel *(noun)* an officer in the army (p. 35)

colony *(noun)* land ruled by another country (p. 6)

Creole *(noun)* someone who is born in South America but has European ancestors (p. 6)

democracy *(noun)* a government in which people choose their leaders in elections (p. 13)

dictator *(noun)* a person who rules a country with complete control (p. 32)

disloyal *(adjective)* dishonest or unfaithful to your friends or country (p. 14)

exile *(noun)* someone who has been sent away from their own country (p. 19)

generation *(noun)* all the people born around the same time (p. 10)

Glossary

governor *(noun)* the person who runs a colony or territory (p. 18)

ideal *(noun)* a dream of something that is perfect (p. 19)

invade *(verb)* to take over a nation by force (p. 16)

lance *(noun)* a long pointed stick used as a weapon (p. 23)

launch *(verb)* to start something new (p. 22)

liberate *(verb)* to set free (p. 18)

passion *(noun)* very strong feelings (p. 12)

plantation *(noun)* a large farm growing crops such as coffee, sugar, or cotton (p. 7)

rebel *(noun)* someone who fights to change the government (p. 13)

revolution *(noun)* an uprising by the people of a country to change their government (p. 10)

rival *(adjective)* competing (p. 31)

swear *(verb)* to promise (p. 16)

Index

Index

Room 212

Q
Quito 24
  liberation of 28

R
Rodríguez, Simón 9,
  12–14,

S
Sáenz, Manuela 32–34,
  36
slavery 7, 12

U
United States 10, 19, 31

V
Venezuela
  liberation of 26